A Paines Plough, Theatr Clwyd &
Orange Tree Theatre Production

HOW TO BE A KID

by Sarah McDonald-Hughes

The first performance of *How To Be A Kid* took place on
24 June 2017 in Paines Plough's Roundabout at Theatr Clwyd

PAINES
PLOUGH

ARTS COUNCIL
ENGLAND

Supported using public funding by
ARTS COUNCIL
ENGLAND

Theatr
Clwyd

Orange
Tree
Theatre

How To Be A Kid

by Sarah McDonald-Hughes

Cast

JOE/BUS DRIVER/TEXTBOOK	Hasan Dixon
MUM/TAYLOR/NAN/ABI/MICHELLE/ MS JOHNSON/McDONALD'S VOICE	Sally Messham
MOLLY	Katie Elin-Salt

Production Team

Direction	James Grieve
Lighting	Peter Small
Sound	Dominic Kennedy
Movement	Jennifer Jackson
Programmer	Joe Izzard
Assistant Director	Emily Ling Williams
Line Producer	Francesca Moody
Dramaturg	Guy Jones
Company Stage Manager	Linnea Fridén Grønning
Technical Stage Manager	Callum Thomson
2nd Technical Stage Manager	Hamish Ellis

SARAH McDONALD-HUGHES (Writer)
Sarah is an actor and writer from Manchester.

Plays include: *Witch*, *Multi Story* (Octagon Bolton/Monkeywood Theatre), *Wondrous Place* (Northern Spirit/Liverpool Unity/Sheffield Crucible/Northern Stage/Royal Exchange), *Flesh* (Monkeywood Theatre/Royal Exchange), *By Far the Greatest Team*, *Once in a House on Fire*, *Maine Road* (Monkeywood Theatre), *Salisbury Street* (Box of Tricks/Liverpool Everyman), *The Tower* (Paines Plough/Royal Exchange Studio), *The Tree*, *Night Train* (Action Transport Theatre), *Our Pals* and *The North* (Royal Exchange Studio).

Radio includes: *A Roof Over Our Hads*, *Dad*, *Take Me To Redcar*, *Maine Road* (BBC Radio 4). Television includes numerous episodes of *Doctors* for BBC1. Sarah works regularly as an actor in theatre, television and radio and is Co-Artistic director of Monkeywood Theatre.

Sarah's play *Blackout* opens at the Dukes, Lancaster in Autumn 2017. Her play *Sherbet*, co-written with Curtis Cole, won the 2017 National Octagon Prize and will be produced at the Octagon Theatre in Spring 2018.

HASAN DIXON (Joe, Bus Driver, Textbook)
Hasan trained at Central School of Speech and Drama.

Theatre includes: *War Horse* (National Theatre); *Carry On Jaywick* (HighTide); *Eventide*, *The Spanish Tragedy* (Arcola); *Re:Home* (The Yard); *Fear of Music* (Up in Arms/Out of Joint); *The Alchemist* (Liverpool Playhouse); *The Glass Menagerie* (Everyman); *Yerma* (Gate/Hull Truck); *You: The Player* (West Yorkshire Playhouse); *Ghosts* (UK tour); *The Return* (Southwark Playhouse).

Film & TV includes: *A Touch of Frost* (ITV); *Doctors*, *Silent Witness*, *Call the Midwife* (BBC); *This Is Not Happening* (Picnic Films) *And John Carter* (Disney/Pixar).

SALLY MESSHAM (Mum, Taylor, Nan, Abi, Michelle, Ms Johnson, McDonald's Voice)
Sally trained at RADA.

Theatre includes: *Tipping the Velvet* (Lyric Hammersmith); *The Sugar Wife*, *Women of Twilight*, *After Miss Julie* (RADA).

Film & TV includes: *Allied* (Gk Films); *Denial* (Krasnoff/Forster Entertainment); *Midwinter of the Spirit* (ITV Studios for ITV); *The Miniaturist* (The Forge Entertainment).

KATIE ELIN-SALT (Molly)
Katie Elin-Salt trained at Royal Welsh College of Music and Drama.

Theatre includes: *Twelfth Night* (Shakespeare's Globe); *A Comedy of Errors* (National Theatre tour); *Crouch Touch Pause Engage* (Out of Joint/National Theatre of Wales); *Symphony* (Nabakov/ Soho); *Under Milk Wood*, *Season's Greetings*, *Educating Rita*, *As You Like It* (Theatr Clwyd); *Snow White and the Seven Dwarves* (Regent Theatre); *Cinderella* (Leeds City Varieties); *The Rise and Fall of Little Voice* (Bolton Octagon); *Holly and Ivan's Christmas Adventure* (Lyric Hammersmith); *Stealing Sweets and Punching People* (Nu-Write); *Love Steals Us From Loneliness* (National Theatre of Wales).

Television includes: *Stella* (Tidy Productions/Sky 1); *Doctors* (BBC TV); *Flash Prank* (Splash Media/MTV); *Tissues and Issues* (BBC); *And Perfect Summer* (Fiction Factory).

JAMES GRIEVE (Direction)
James is Joint Artistic Director of Paines Plough. He was formerly co-founder and Artistic Director of nabokov, and Associate Director of the Bush Theatre.

For Paines Plough James has directed *The Angry Brigade* by James Graham, *Broken Biscuits* and *Jumpers for Goalposts* by Tom Wells, *Hopelessly Devoted* and *Wasted* by Kate Tempest, *An Intervention* and *Love, Love, Love* by Mike Bartlett, *Fly Me To The Moon* by Marie Jones, *Tiny Volcanoes* by Laurence Wilson, *You Cannot Go Forward From Where You Are Right Now* by David Watson, *The Sound of Heavy Rain* by Penelope Skinner, *Organised* by Lucinda Burnett and *Happiness* by Nick Payne for BBC Radio 3. Further credits include a new production of *Les Misérables* for Wermland Opera in Karlstad, Sweden; *Translations* (Sheffield Theatres/ETT/Rose – winner Best Production, UK Theatre Awards 2014); *66 Books: A Nobody* by Laura Dockrill, *The Whisky Taster* by James Graham, *St Petersburg* by Declan Feenan and *Psychogeography* by Lucy Kirkwood (Bush); *Artefacts* by Mike Bartlett (nabokov/Bush, national tour & Off-Broadway); *Kitchen*, *Bedtime for Bastards* and *Nikolina* by Van Badham (nabokov).

PETER SMALL (Lighting)
Peter studied Lighting Design at The Royal Academy of Dramatic Art.

Musical theatre includes: *Cinderella* (Loughborough Theatre); *Tom & Jerry* (EventBox Theatre, Egypt); *All or Nothing* (UK national tours/Crescent/Vaults); *The Venus Factor* (Bridewell).

Theatre includes: *Bard on Board* (Cunard Queen Mary 2); *A Midsummer Night's Dream* (Forum Alpbach, Austria); *In the Gut* (Brighton Festival/Blue Elephant Theatre/Clown Fest 2016); *Electric* (Rio Cinema); *Our Teacher is a Troll* (UK tour/ Paines Plough); *She Called Me Mother* (UK tours); *Crazy Lady, Free Association* (Forum Alpbach); *East End Boys and West End Girls* (Arcola/UK tour); *Politrix* (Hackney Showroom); *Almost Near* (Finborough); *Richard III* (Cunard Queen Mary 2); *The Witch of Edmonton* (Vanbrugh Theatre); *The Daughter-in-Law* (George Bernard Shaw Theatre); *Mother Theresa is Dead* (Gielgud).

Dance includes: *STEPLive! 2016* (Sadler's Wells); *STEPLive! 2017* (Royal Festival Hall); *A Night with Gravity Circus* (Jacksons Lane).

Concerts include: *A Night With Jason Robert Brown* (Royal Festival Hall).

Events include: *The Art of the Steal* (Louisa Guinness Gallery); *Never Such Innocence* (Australia House).

Associate/Assistant/Relight work includes: *Tiger Bay* (Cape Town Opera/ Wales Millennium Centre); *Everybody's Talking About Jamie* (Sheffield Crucible); *Love, Lies and Taxidermy* (Theatre Clwyd); *Kiss Me Kate* (Théâtre du Châtelet/Grand Theatre Luxembourg); *Pink Confetti* (Babel International Festival); *Gianni Schicchi* (Teatro Real Opera House); *East is East* (Trafalgar Studios 1); *Thérèse Raquin* (Park/Finborough); *Arabian Nights* (Cunard Queen Mary 2); *The Realness* (Hackney Show Rooms).

DOMINIC KENNEDY (Sound)
Dominic Kennedy is a Sound Designer and Music Producer for performance and live events, he has a keen interest in developing new work and implementing sound and music at an early stage in a creative process. Dominic is a graduate from Royal Central School of Speech and Drama where he developed specialist skills in collaborative and devised theatre making, music composition and installation practices. His work often fuses found sound, field recordings, music composition and synthesis. Dominic has recently designed for and collaborated with Paines Plough, Engineer, Goat and Monkey, Jamie Wood, Gameshow, Manchester Royal Exchange, Outbox, Jemima James and Mars Tarrab. Recent installation work includes interactive sound design for *Gingerline* (pop-up restaurant pioneers) and the launch of Terry Pratchett's *The Shepherd's Crown*. Recent design credits include: *Broken Biscuits* (Paines Plough/Live Theatre Newcastle/nationwide tour); *Growth* (Paines Plough/nationwide

tour); *Love, Lies and Taxidermy* (Paines Plough/Theatr Clwyd/Sherman Theatre/nationwide tour); *I Got Superpowers For My Birthday* (Paines Plough/Half Moon/nationwide tour); *With a Little Bit of Luck* (Paines Plough/Latitude Festival/nationwide tour); *The Human Ear* (Paines Plough/ nationwide tour); *The Devil Speaks True* (nationwide tour); *Run* (New Diorama); *Ono* (Soho); *Crocodiles* (Manchester Royal Exchange).

JENNIFER JACKSON (Movement)
Jennifer trained at East 15 and is a movement director and actor. Movement direction includes: *The Mountaintop* (Young Vic); *Death of a Salesman* (Royal & Derngate); *The Ugly One* (Park); *Phone Home* (Shoreditch Town Hall); *Why the Whales Came* (Southbank Centre); *Wuthering Heights* (workshop – Manchester Royal Exchange); *Stone Face* (Finborough); *Debris* (Southwark Playhouse/OpenWorks); *Macbeth* (Sam Wanamaker Playhouse/Passion in Practice); *Silent Planet* (Finborough); *Pericles* (Berwaldhallen, Stockholm); *Subterranean Sepoys* (New Diorama); *The Future* (The Yard); *Other (Please Specify)*; *Atoms* (Company Three); *Takeover 2017* (Tricycle). Jennifer was the assistant movement director to Kate Sagovsky on the Paines Plough Roundabout season 2014 (Fringe First Winners), and is an associate artist with OpenWorks Theatre, Upstart Theatre, and a member of Tangled Feet.

As a performer Jennifer has worked with the NT, NT Studio, BAC, Bath Theatre Royal, Royal & Derngate Theatre, Sam Wanamaker Playhouse, Theatre 503, Arcola, Openworks Theatre, Derby Theatre, The Yard, The Harold Pinter Theatre (West End), Southwark Playhouse, Bervaldhallen (Stockholm), Lucas Theatre (Savannah, USA), Pearl Theatre (New York).

EMILY LING WILLIAMS (Assistant Director)
Emily was the assistant director on *The Island Nation* (Arcola, 2016). She completed Introduction to Directing and Springboard at The Young Vic during which she directed *Lungs* (Platform/ Young Vic, 2016).

Emily has read scripts for Heyday Films, Origin Pictures and Blueprint Pictures.

She trained on the Acting Foundation Course at RADA before graduating from UCL with a BA in Philosophy.

Alongside directing she is also doing an MSc in Comparative Political Thought at SOAS and is on the Soho Theatre Writers Lab.

PAINES PLOUGH

Paines Plough is the UK's national theatre of new plays. We commission and produce the best playwrights and tour their plays far and wide. Whether you're in Liverpool or Lyme Regis, Scarborough or Southampton, a Paines Plough show is coming to a theatre near you soon.

'The lifeblood of the UK's theatre ecosystem' *Guardian*

Paines Plough was formed in 1974 over a pint of Paines bitter in the Plough pub. Since then we've produced more than 170 new productions by world renowned playwrights like Stephen Jeffreys, Abi Morgan, Sarah Kane, Mark Ravenhill, Dennis Kelly and Mike Bartlett. We've toured those plays to hundreds of places from Manchester to Moscow to Maidenhead.

'That noble company Paines Plough, de facto national theatre of new writing' *Daily Telegraph*

Over the last two years we've produced 22 shows and performed them in 180 places across four continents. We tour to more than 30,000 people a year from Cornwall to the Orkney Islands; in village halls and Off-Broadway, at music festivals and student unions, online and on radio, and in our own pop-up theatre Roundabout.

With Programme 2017 we continue to tour the length and breadth of the UK from clubs and pubs to lakeside escapes and housing estates. Roundabout hosts a jam-packed Edinburgh Festival Fringe programme and brings mini-festivals to each stop on its nationwide tour, and you can even catch us on screen with *Every Brilliant Thing* available on Sky Atlantic and HBO.

'I think some theatre just saved my life' @kate_clement on Twitter

PAINES PLOUGH — ROUNDABOUT

'A beautifully designed masterpiece in engineering… a significant breakthrough in theatre technology.' *The Stage*

Roundabout is Paines Plough's beautiful portable in-the-round theatre. It's a completely self-contained 168-seat auditorium that flat packs into a single lorry and pops up anywhere from theatres to school halls, sports centres, warehouses, car parks and fields.

We built Roundabout to enable us to tour to places that don't have theatres. For the next decade Roundabout will travel the length and breadth of the UK bringing the nation's best playwrights and a thrilling theatrical experience to audiences everywhere.

Over the last three years Roundabout has toured to 17 places, hosted 1,600 hours of entertainment for more than 65,000 people.

Roundabout was designed by Lucy Osborne and Emma Chapman at Studio Three Sixty in collaboration with Charcoalblue and Howard Eaton.

WINNER of Theatre Building of the Year at The Stage Awards 2014

'Roundabout venue wins most beautiful interior venue by far @edfringe.'
@ChaoticKirsty on Twitter

'Roundabout is a beautiful, magical space. Hidden tech make it Turkish-bath-tranquil but with circus-tent-cheek. Aces.'
@evenicol on Twitter

Roundabout was made possible thanks to the belief and generous support of the following Trusts and individuals and all who named a seat in Roundabout. We thank them all.

TRUSTS AND FOUNDATIONS
Andrew Lloyd Webber Foundation
Paul Hamlyn Foundation
Garfield Weston Foundation
J Paul Getty Jnr Charitable Trust
John Ellerman Foundation

CORPORATE
Universal Consolidated Group
Howard Eaton Lighting Ltd
Charcoalblue
Avolites Ltd
Factory Settings
Total Solutions

Pop your name on a seat and help us pop-up around the UK:
www.justgiving.com/fundraising/roundaboutauditorium

www.painesplough.com/roundabout
#roundaboutpp

Paines Plough

Joint Artistic Directors	James Grieve
	George Perrin
Senior Producer	Hanna Streeter
General Manager	Aysha Powell
Producer	Francesca Moody
Assistant Producer	Sofia Stephanou
Administrator	Simone Ibbett-Brown
Marketing and Audience	
Development Officer	Jack Heaton
Production Assistant	Harriet Bolwell
Finance and Admin Assistant	Charlotte Walton
Technical Director	Colin Everitt
Trainee Director	Emily Ling Williams
Production Placement	Alexandra Sikkink
Marketing Placement	Anushka Chakravarti
Admin Placement	Yuhan Zhang
Channel 4 Playwright in Residence	Zia Ahmed
Press Representative	The Corner Shop
Graphic Designer	Michael Windsor-Ungureanu
	Thread Design

Board of Directors

Caro Newling (Chair), Kim Grant, Nia Janis, Dennis Kelly, Matthew Littleford, Anne McMeehan, Christopher Millard, Cindy Polemis and Andrea Stark.

Paines Plough Limited is a company limited by guarantee and a registered charity.
Registered Company no: 1165130
Registered Charity no: 267523

Paines Plough, 4th Floor, 43 Aldwych, London WC2B 4DN
+ 44 (0) 20 7240 4533
office@painesplough.com
www.painesplough.com

 Follow @PainesPlough on Twitter

 Like Paines Plough at facebook.com/PainesPloughHQ

 Follow @painesplough on Instagram

Donate to Paines Plough at justgiving.com/PainesPlough

Theatr
Clwyd

'One of the hidden treasures of North Wales, a huge vibrant culture complex' *Guardian*

Theatr Clwyd is one of the foremost producing theatres in Wales – a beacon of excellence looking across the Clwydian Hills yet only forty minutes from Liverpool.

Since 1976 we have been a theatrical powerhouse and much-loved home for our community. Now, led by Tamara Harvey and Liam Evans-Ford, we are going from strength to strength producing world-class theatre, from new plays to classic revivals.

We have three theatres, a cinema, café, bar and art galleries and, alongside our own shows, offer a rich and varied programme of visual arts, film, theatre, music, dance and comedy. We also work extensively with our local community, schools and colleges and create award-winning work for, with and by young people. In our fortieth year we will have co-produced with the Wales Millennium Centre, Sherman Theatre, Gagglebabble and The Other Room in Cardiff, Paines Plough, Vicky Graham Productions at the Yard Theatre, High Tide, Hampstead Theatre, Bristol Old Vic, The Rose Theatre, Kingston, Headlong and Sheffield Theatres.

Over 200,000 people a year come through our doors and in 2015 Theatr Clwyd was voted the Most Welcoming Theatre in Wales.

ARTISTIC DIRECTOR Tamara Harvey
EXECUTIVE DIRECTOR Liam Evans-Ford
ASSOCIATE PRODUCER William James
ASSISTANT PRODUCER Nick Stevenson
THEATRE ADMINISTRATOR Melanie Jones
EXECUTIVE ASSISTANT Tracy Waters
CAPITAL DEVELOPMENT ASSOCIATE Pat Nelder

CREATIVE ENGAGEMENT
DIRECTOR OF CREATIVE ENGAGEMENT Gwennan Mair Jones
CREATIVE ENGAGEMENT ASSOCIATE Emyr John
CREATIVE ENGAGEMENT CO-ORDINATOR Nerys Edwards
TUTORS Laura Heap, Liz Morris, Clare-Louise Rhys-Jones
SUPPORT WORKERS Chris Ablett, Phoebe Dacre, Dave Humphreys, Gaenor Williams

DEVELOPMENT
DIRECTOR OF DEVELOPMENT Daniel Porter-Jones
SPONSORSHIP MANAGER Annie Dayson

FINANCE
DIRECTOR OF FINANCE Emma Sullivan
FINANCE CO-ORDINATOR Sandra Almeida
FINANCE ASSISTANT Carol Parsonage

GALLERIES
GALLERY CURATOR Jonathan Le Vay

MARKETING AND COMMUNICATIONS
DIRECTOR OF MARKETING AND COMMUNICATIONS Sam Freeman

SALES MANAGER Marie Thorpe
PRESS AND COMMUNICATIONS COORDINATOR Anthony Timothy
DIGITAL AND COMMUNICATIONS COORDINATOR Angharad Madog
DESIGN AND DIGITAL ASSISTANT Crayg Ward
SALES MERCHANDISER Carole Jones
SALES ASSISTANTS Deborah Charles, Catrin Davies, Carol Edwards, Elaine Godwin, Gwennan Henstock, Rosemary Hughes, Rhiannon Isaac, Nikki Jones, Angela Peters, Jean Proctor, Ann Phillips, Lyn Rush, Jennifer Walters

PRODUCTION
DIRECTOR of PRODUCTION Jim Davis
PRODUCTION MANAGER Hannah Lobb
TECHNICAL MANAGER Geoff Farmer
SENIOR TECHNICIAN (STAGE) Nick Samuel
TECHNICIANS (STAGE) Paul Adams, Angel Hasted
SENIOR TECHNICIAN (LIGHTING AND SOUND) Chris Skinner
TECHNICIANS (LIGHTING AND SOUND) David Powell, Neil Queripel, Nathan Stewart, Matthew Williams, Neil Williams
TECHNICAL APPRENTICES James Davison, Joe McDermott
WARDROBE MANAGER Deborah Knight
WARDROBE CUTTERS Emma Aldridge Michal Shyne
WARDROBE ASSISTANT Alison Hartnell
COSTUME MAINTENANCE Amber Davies, Karen Jones
WORKSHOP MANAGER Steve Eccleson

WORKSHOP ASSISTANTS Dave Davies, Andy Sutters
PROPS MAKER Bob Heaton
SCENIC ARTIST Mike Jones

OPERATIONS
DIRECTOR OF OPERATIONS Andrew Roberts
DUTY FRONT OF HOUSE MANAGERS Laura Gray, Gwennan Henstock
OPERATIONS COORDINATOR Andy Reilly
OPERATIONS ADMINISTRATOR Sarah Eldridge
EVENTS COORDINATOR Nathan Stewart
CHEF Richard Hughes
SOUS CHEF Tina Lane
FOOD & DRINK SUPERVISOR Salvatore Vena
OPERATIONS TEAM LEADER Callum Roberts
BAR ASSISTANTS Carol Williams, Andrew Walls, Matthew Wright, Delyth Williams, Daryl Batchelor, Gwennan Henstock, Andrew Hughes, Stewart Hazledoen
CATERING ASSISTANTS Rachel Wilday, Ann Phillips, Callum Selvester, Callum Roberts, Dave Humphreys, Kim Holsgrove, Rhiannon Isaac, Kizi Lane, Enya Maguire, Jana Fabianova
MERCHANDISE ASSISTANTS Luisa Sciarillo, Carol Williams, Delyth Williams
CINEMA CO-ORDINATOR Mike Roberts
PROJECTIONISTS Sam Davidson, Matthew Wright
BUILDING SERVICES COORDINATOR Jim Scarratt
GREEN ROOM Clare Brown, Carol Ann Jones, Caroline Jones
AUDIO DESCRIBERS Trevor Dennis, Margaret Jones, Jon Payne, Diana Stebbing

Orange Tree Theatre

At its home in Richmond, South West London, the **Orange Tree Theatre** aims to entertain, challenge, move and amaze with a bold and continually evolving mix of new and rediscovered plays in our unique in-the-round space. We want to change lives by telling remarkable stories from a wide variety of times and places, filtered through the singular imagination of our writers and the remarkable close-up presence of our actors.

Over its forty-five-year history the Orange Tree has had an exceptional track record in discovering writers and promoting their early work, as well as rediscovering artists from the past whose work had either been disregarded or forgotten.

In the last two years, the OT has been recognised for its work with sixteen major industry awards, including ten Offies (Off West End Awards), three UK Theatre Awards, the Alfred Fagon Audience Award and the Peter Brook Empty Space Award.

In 2016 the Orange Tree's work was seen in twenty-four other towns and cities across the country.

The OT is proud to be co-producing *Black Mountain* by Brad Birch, *Out of Love* by Elinor Cook and *How To Be a Kid* by Sarah McDonald-Hughes in the Roundabout season with Paines Plough and Theatr Clwyd. In Edinburgh, the OT's co-production with Farnham Maltings of *Jess and Joe Forever* by Zoe Cooper is at the Traverse Theatre.

The Orange Tree is a registered charity (no. 266128) whose mission is to enable audiences to experience the next generation of theatre talent, experiment with ground-breaking new drama and explore the plays of the past the have inspired the theatremakers of the present. To find out how you can help us to do that you can visit **orangetreetheatre.co.uk/discover**

Generously supported by the London Borough of Richmond upon Thames.

orangetreetheatre.co.uk | @OrangeTreeThtr | Facebook/Instagram: OrangeTreeTheatre

Artistic Director	Paul Miller
Executive Director	Sarah Nicholson
Development Director	Alex Jones
Technical Manager	Stuart Burgess
Education Director	Imogen Bond
Theatre Manager	Nicola Courtenay
Finance Manager	Caroline Goodwin
General Manager	Rebecca Murphy
Press & Marketing Manager	Ben Clare
Development Manager	Rebecca Frater
Literary Associate	Guy Jones
Production Technician	Lisa Berrystone
Development Officer	Emma Kendall
Education and Participation Assistant	Izzy Cotterill

AT THE ORANGE TREE THEATRE

7 SEPTEMBER – 7 OCTOBER 2017
An Orange Tree Theatre production in association with Up in Arms
The March on Russia
By David Storey

10 – 28 OCTOBER 2017
A Paines Plough and Pentabus Theatre Company production
Every Brilliant Thing
By Duncan Macmillan with Jonny Donahoe

2 NOVEMBER–2 DECEMBER 2017
An Orange Tree Theatre production
Poison
By Lot Vekemans
Translated by Rina Vergano

7 DEC 2017–20 JAN 2018
An Orange Tree Theatre production
Misalliance
By Bernard Shaw

20 DEC 2017–6 JAN 2018
A Wizard Presents, Orange Tree Theatre and Little Angel Theatre
co-production
Kika's Birthday
By Danyah and John Miller

HOW TO BE A KID

A play for seven- to eleven-year-olds

Sarah McDonald-Hughes

2

Characters

MOLLY, *twelve*
JOE, *six*
MUM

NAN
TAYLOR
BUS DRIVER
ABI
TEXTBOOK
MICHELLE
MS JOHNSON
McDONALD'S ASSISTANT
CLEANER

All characters can be played by the three actors playing
MOLLY, MUM *and* JOE.

*This text went to press before the end of rehearsals and so may
differ slightly from the play as performed.*

Music: 'Shake It Off' by Taylor Swift.

MOLLY *and* TAYLOR (MOLLY's *friend, not Taylor Swift*) *burst into the space. They dance their routine to the music, having a great time. They are really good.*

The music fades. They stop and look at each other: it's time to go.

MOLLY. I'll miss you.

TAYLOR. You're going home.

MOLLY. I know.

TAYLOR. It's going to be amazing.

MOLLY. I know.

TAYLOR. You best not forget me.

MOLLY. As if. You best not forget me.

TAYLOR. As if.

Beat.

See you then, Molly.

TAYLOR *backs away from* MOLLY. *Before she disappears, she puts her finger to the side of her head and taps it.* MOLLY *does the same back to* TAYLOR.

TAYLOR *disappears.* MOLLY *shouts after her.*

MOLLY. Taylor! Taylor, come back! I need to ask you something!

Nothing.

TAYLOR! What am I... what am I going to do without you?

Beat.

So, okay, it's Sunday afternoon and I am holding a black bin bag containing all my stuff and I am standing outside a house. It's a house I haven't seen for a long time – a house I haven't seen for five weeks and one day.

It looks just the same. There's the same broken blue gate and Joe's same old green scooter in the front garden and the same grey curtains in the same window and the same red front door opens.

CREAK. MOLLY*'s* MUM *appears*.

And then… there she is. (*To* MUM.) Mum!

MUM. Molly!

MOLLY. Mum.

MUM. Love.

MOLLY. Hiya.

MUM. My Supergirl. Come in.

They go inside.

MOLLY (*to us*). Supergirl. That's just a thing that my mum and my nan called me when I was little. For a while I thought I was an actual superhero with magical powers and I used to pretend to like rescue things and fly and stuff but then I got older and I realised that there's actually no such thing as superheroes and I was just a normal girl. Which was disappointing.

MUM. My Molly.

MOLLY (*to us*). Mum looks… normal.

Beat.

MUM. I've done us a cake –

MOLLY. A cake?

MUM. What's wrong with that? Look –

MOLLY (*to us*). This is not normal. Nan used to make us cakes but never Mum. It's a yellow cake with jam inside. It's a bit brown on top but I go – (*To* MUM.) Mmmmmmm.

MOLLY *goes to the window, looks up and down the street.*

Where's Joe?

MUM. His dad's dropping him off after swimming. Any minute now.

MOLLY (*to us*). I don't know why but for some reason, it feels like things will be okay when Joe gets back. Then, things will go back to normal. I mean he's a pain, Joe, he's extremely extremely annoying but he's also kind of useful. (*Beat.*) Don't tell him I said that.

MOLLY *keeps looking out of the window for* JOE.

MUM (*clocking* MOLLY*'s gaze*). I know, poor Vera looks a bit miserable, doesn't she? I'm going to put an ad in the *Evening News* this week.

MOLLY. You can't sell Vera!

MUM. Your nan wouldn't want her sitting there getting sad and rusty, would she? She'd want someone to get some use out of her.

MOLLY. She was Nan's best friend!

MUM. Sweetheart, Vera's a car. And we could do with the money.

MOLLY. I could have her. When I'm older.

MUM. I doubt she'll be running by then. She's on her last legs as it is.

MOLLY (*to us*). Actually, I can already drive. My mum doesn't know this, obviously. Taylor taught me in the car park of B&M one night when Kyle's brother came down in his car and let us all have a go. It's actually not that hard, once you get the hang.

MUM. Come on, Moll, come away from the window. Let me look at you.

MOLLY *steps towards* MUM. MUM *stares at her, smiling.*

There you are.

MOLLY *dithers, puts her arms out and turns in a circle.*
MUM *watches.*

MOLLY. And there I am. Standing in the kitchen of a house that looks like my house but somehow doesn't feel like my house any more, with a mum who looks like my mum but is actually a kind of new, shiny, smiley, fixed-up Mum.

I want to stop turning round but I don't know if I should, so I keep going, around and around like the little ballerina in my nan's jewellery box, but then –

JOE*'s music – fast and loud.*

JOE. I'M BACK!

JOE *runs in fast, stops in front of* MUM, *hugs her.*

MUM. Joe!

JOE. Mum!

JOE *and* MUM *hold each other.*

MOLLY. Joe's my little brother. He's six –

JOE (*to* MOLLY). Hey! I'll say it. I can do my own bit –

MOLLY (*tutting*). Fine –

(*To us.*) This is what he's like.

JOE. I'm Joe. I'm six, and my favourite dinosaur is a Triceratops –

MOLLY (*to us*). Changes every week –

JOE. And I live at number twenty-two, Thornton Road –

MOLLY (*to us*). He's a bit like a puppy, he'll calm down in a bit –

JOE (*to* MUM). Hey, Mum, Mum, Mum, watch this –

JOE *does a forward roll and stands up again quickly after.*

MUM. Wow, Joe –

JOE. Learned it when I was at Dad's –

MUM. S'brilliant that, son –

JOE. And I learned what one add two add three add four is! It's
ten! It's ten, Mum, it's ten!

MOLLY. See what I mean? He wants to do everything that I
can do –

JOE. I don't!

MOLLY. – even though I'm six years older than him so he
can't –

JOE. I can!

MOLLY. When he was three he had to go to hospital because he
copied me jumping off the settee pretending to fly and
cracked his head on his toy garage. So when we got home, in
secret, I taught him to do it properly:

MOLLY *is nine,* JOE *is three.*

Ready? When I say go, jump to me, right? One, two, three –

JOE *jumps.* MOLLY *helps him land.*

JOE. Did it!

MOLLY. I never said go, you were supposed to wait –

JOE. I flying!

MOLLY. You could've hurt yourself again –

JOE. I Supergirl –

MOLLY. No, I'm Supergirl! You can be Superboy if you like.
Supergirl's helper.

JOE. I Superboy!

Back to now.

MOLLY. At least Joe is the same.

JOE. What's for tea? Can we have McDonald's?

MOLLY. Joe loves McDonald's.

JOE. And you do –

MOLLY. Yeah only I'm twelve now so I call it Maccie D's.

JOE. Wow, my room! My dinosaurs! My trainset!

MOLLY. Joe hasn't played with his trains since he was three –

JOE. I have –

MOLLY. He's just overexcited –

JOE. I'm not –

MOLLY. Nan used to call him a loose cannon –

NAN. He's a loose cannon, our Joe –

JOE. Is that a CAKE?

MOLLY. He loves cake.

JOE. I love cake!

   They eat the cake.

   No one speaks. They all just eat.

MUM. More cake, anyone?

JOE. Yeah!

MOLLY. No thanks.

MUM. What was the food like at Riverside?

MOLLY. The pizza's alright but the stew is disgusting. Me and
   Taylor sit there begging her for toast and peanut butter
   instead.

MUM. Who's Taylor?

MOLLY (*to us*). I told her this. (*To* MUM.) I told you. She's my
   best friend.

MUM. I thought what's-her-name from school was your best
   friend?

JOE. Abi!

MUM. Yes, Abi –

MOLLY. I don't know now.

(*To us*.) Abi was my best friend. But then I met Taylor.

MUM. That's okay. You can have lots of friends, can't you? And Taylor, is she still at Riverside, love?

MOLLY. Yeah.

MUM. Oh.

MOLLY (*to us*). Seventeen miles away from our estate and you can't get there on a bus. We checked. Me and Taylor printed off a map in Yvonne's office showing the way from Riverside to mine. Basically you need a car.

MUM. Look at you, both of you. I'm so happy to have you both back here, where you belong.

MOLLY *is in bed*.

MOLLY (*to us*). But when I'm lying in my bed, with One Direction and Little Mix and Rihanna and Taylor Swift looking down on me… I can't get comfy. It's like I don't fit like I used to.

I'm home. But somehow it doesn't feel right. And I can feel this sort of wriggling, squirmy feeling in my tummy, a kind of worry feeling that won't go away.

It feels like a sort of… worm.

And I know I should be happy to be home but I wish that I could creep down the corridor in my pyjamas, knock on Taylor's door, jump in her bed and whisper until Yvonne comes round and catches me.

Taylor. I've known her five weeks and one day and in that time I've learnt every single thing about her. She's my best ever best friend.

She's kind of… glowy, as if someone's left a light on inside of her, as if she's magical. You can't help staring at her, see what she's going to do next.

The first time I met her, she actually read my mind. For real.

So, okay. I'm walking into the TV room at Riverside.
Yvonne is talking, telling me everyone's names

YVONNE. This is Reece and Curtis, boys, say hello to Molly,
please –

BOYS (*daft*). Hello to Molly please!

MOLLY. But I'm not listening, I'm looking round and
wondering how I can stay here, without my mum and Joe.

A green carpet with swirls on.

A big-screen TV and two boys fighting over the remote.

YVONNE. Reece, Curtis, enough!

MOLLY. They don't even look up. Yvonne goes over to sort
them out and I'm standing there, feeling stupid, on my own.

And then I see her.

She's sitting on the corner of the orange settee dodging the
kicks. Her face is scrunched up, as if she wants to get off the
settee but she won't let them win.

And she looks at me.

She looks at me as if she can see right into my head, as if she
can see all my brain and my insides and my thoughts and
everything.

And what I'm thinking is

MOLLY *and* TAYLOR *are in Riverside. They stand at the
edges of the room, far apart.*

TAYLOR. 'I can't live here.'

MOLLY. What?

TAYLOR. That's totally what you're thinking. 'I can't live
here.'

MOLLY. How do you know?

TAYLOR. Just tell. And it's what I thought when I walked in. You'll get used to it. I'm Taylor.

BOYS (*mimicking*). I'm Taylor!

MOLLY (*to us*). Then they fall about laughing. But Taylor just turns round and goes –

TAYLOR. Shut it. (*To* MOLLY.) Sorry about that. Shall we get out of here? (*So only* MOLLY *can hear.*) I know where the hot chocolate is.

MOLLY (*to us*). So she shows me round. Doesn't take long. It's not big, Riverside, it's kind of like a cross between a house and a tiny school.

TAYLOR *hands* MOLLY *a hot chocolate.*

TAYLOR. Hot chocolate. Yvonne hides it behind the Weetabix or the boys would get through it in a day. So. What else? There's only two girls – me and you – and three boys. Reece, Curtis and Kyle. Or, Idiot One, Idiot Two and Idiot Three, as I like to call them. Joke. They're alright. Is this your first time?

MOLLY. What?

TAYLOR. In care?

MOLLY. Yeah. How about you?

TAYLOR *laughs.*

TAYLOR. No. Ask me how many places I been in.

MOLLY. How many places have you been in?

TAYLOR. Twenty-two.

MOLLY. Wow.

TAYLOR. Fourteen foster placements and eight children's centres. Not that many really. Reece has been in thirty-six.

MOLLY. Right.

TAYLOR. Been in care since I was eight.

MOLLY. How come?

TAYLOR. You're not supposed to ask that.

MOLLY. Sorry.

TAYLOR. I might not want to talk about it.

MOLLY. No, sorry.

TAYLOR. It's alright. My nan died and my mum can't look after me.

MOLLY. My nan died.

TAYLOR. And your mum can't look after you?

MOLLY. She's in hospital.

TAYLOR. So you ended up here.

MOLLY. Soon as she's better I'm going back.

TAYLOR. Right. I'm not even meant to be here.

MOLLY. How come?

TAYLOR. Had a foster placement but it fell through. They're trying to find me another one but till they do… What music you in to?

MOLLY (*quickly*). Little Mix, Beyoncé, One Direction, Rihanna, Katy Perry, Taylor Swift – I love Taylor Swift –

Music. They dance – a routine.

(*To us.*) Every night, I sneak into her room so we can talk when we're meant to be asleep.

Sometimes we do fall asleep and I don't wake up till Yvonne comes round.

MOLLY *sleeps.* TAYLOR *disappears.*

Alarm clock. MUM *jumps up.*

MUM. Molly! Joe! Breakfast's ready!

MOLLY *wakes with a start.*

MOLLY (*half-asleep*). Taylor?

JOE. Wow! Pancakes! Moll! Get down here! There's pancakes!

MOLLY. And then I remember.

> *She goes downstairs.*

> There's pancakes and syrup and bright-red raspberries and orange juice and a Kelloggs Variety Pack and toast and strawberry jam and Mum, wearing an apron I've never seen before.

MUM. Come on, sleepyhead! Sit down, eat up!

MOLLY. Wow, Mum.

JOE. I love pancakes!

MUM. Good lad. Come on, Moll –

MOLLY (*to us*). So we eat pancakes and syrup and Frosties and then we go to school.

> MOLLY *and* JOE *get on the bus.*

BUS DRIVER. Move down the bus!

MOLLY. At school I don't say a single word all morning and then I sit with Abi at lunch.

ABI. So what do you think?

MOLLY. About what?

ABI. Have you not been listening?

MOLLY. Yeah, course –

ABI. So which would you get? The pink or the black?

MOLLY. Um… the black?

ABI (*sighing*). I know but I love the pink.

MOLLY. Pink then.

ABI (*huffing off*). Oh, just forget it!

MOLLY (*to us*). The thing about Abi is that she thinks she's really grown up when actually, she's just a kid. She doesn't even know I was at Riverside at all. I used to get the taxi to drop me off up the road and then walk in as if I'd just got off my old bus.

And I've got away with it, so, you know, cool... but it's actually pretty weird that everyone at school thinks I'm totally normal and just like before when I'm not.

MOLLY. After school, I pick Joe up. Joe never worries about being cool.

They walk home.

JOE. In Show and Tell, I told Ms Morahan that Mum's back and she said that's good. And I said about cake for tea and pancakes for breakfast and –

MOLLY. You shouldn't tell people all that stuff –

JOE. Why not?

MOLLY. We don't want people knowing all our business.

JOE. I do. I like it. I want them to know I'm Joe and I have pancakes and syrup and raspberries!

MOLLY. Stop shouting, will you? Everyone's staring!

JOE. Moll, watch this! I'm a Pterodactyl! – Moll, watch! I can properly do it, wait –

JOE does a dinosaur flight down the street.

They reach the front door. They both stop.

MOLLY (*to us*). We see the front door and we stop.

Key in the lock.

Click.

Quiet.

JOE (*to us*). Nothing. (*Calling.*) Mum?

MOLLY. Mum?

MUM *appears, bright.*

MUM. Kids! Is that the time?

MOLLY. Four o'clock.

MUM. Oh! Silly me.

JOE. Can I put the telly on?

MUM. Course, course, I'll just clear up a little bit, I lost track of time! But you two sit down, and I'll see what's for tea –

MOLLY. What's for tea is beans on toast, only there's no bread so we have crackers. Beans on crackers.

JOE (*through a mouthful of food*). It's amazing! (*To* MUM.) I love it, is there more?

MOLLY. I do not love beans and crackers. But when my mum says –

MUM. Alright, Moll?

MOLLY *does a huge smile and thumbs-up to* MUM.

MOLLY. Homework –

TEXTBOOK. 'The frequency table shows the number of children in the families of some Year 7 students. Work out the mean number of children per family' –

MOLLY. Mum, what's the mean?

MUM. What's what mean?

JOE. Mean is when someone's not very nice to someone else, like if you go, 'Do you want to play dinosaurs?' and they go, 'No because dinosaurs are stupid,' or something like that –

MOLLY. Never mind –

Mum forgets the bath. I have a wash at the sink. Joe doesn't bother.

JOE. Get in! No bath, no bath, no bath, no –

MOLLY. Teeth. Joe! Teeth!

JOE. Hate teeth. Hate teeth, hate teeth, hate teeth –

MOLLY. Open your mouth and keep still!

MOLLY *brushes* JOE*'s teeth.*

Bed.

MUM. Sleep tight, mind the bedbugs don't bite!

MOLLY. That's what my nan used to say.

NAN. Sleep tight, mind the bedbugs don't bite!

MOLLY. And then me and Joe would be lying in bed and she'd go –

NAN. Do you want a story from a book or from Nan's head?

MOLLY *and* JOE. Nan's head!

NAN. Once upon a time, Nan and Vera set off on a fantastic adventure –

MOLLY (*to us*). Every night it was Nan and Vera setting off on a fantastic adventure, doing things she knew we'd love – like flying and going to Maccie D's. I wonder what story she'd tell tonight?

NAN. Molly Daydream, enough stories, time for sleep, we'll have more adventures tomorrow. Close your little peepers and off you go…

MOLLY *closes her eyes and tries to sleep.*

MOLLY (*to us*). But I can't do it. It's like I've forgotten how to sleep in this bed.

MOLLY *creeps into* JOE*'s room.*

Joe?

Nothing.

Joe?

She goes to him and peels one of his eyelids back.

JOE *jumps and screams.*

JOE. AAAAAARRRGH!

MOLLY. AAAAAARRRGH!

JOE (*to us*). I wasn't asleep! (*To* MOLLY.) HA! Made you
jump, made you jump –

MOLLY. Idiot!

JOE. I can't get to sleep. I've been trying and trying but I think
I had too many beans on crackers. They're keeping me up.

MOLLY. I can't sleep either. I keep thinking about Nan.

JOE. Wish she was here.

MOLLY. Me too. She'd know what to do.

(*To us.*) And I do wish she was here but I'm mad with her
too. Because basically, everything, all of this, started with
Nan. It started when Nan got a cough.

They look at each other.

JOE (*to us*). Nan gets a cough.

MOLLY. It doesn't go away.

JOE *coughs.*

It gets worse and worse and Nan stops getting out of her
chair

JOE. And then she stops getting out of bed.

MOLLY. And then she goes to hospital –

MOLLY *and* JOE *make the 'nee-nar' sound of the
ambulance going to hospital.*

JOE. And in hospital it's great! She's always got loads of sweets
and she's got this brilliant bed where you press a button and
it goes up and down –

JOE *goes up and down on the hospital bed.*

MOLLY. And then she gets even worse

JOE. And we aren't allowed to go to see her any more

MOLLY. And then one morning Mum comes home from the hospital and hugs us too tight

JOE. So that it's hard to breathe

MOLLY. And then she stops hugging and she says

Beat.

MUM. I'm so sorry, kids, but I'm afraid that you aren't going to see your nan again.

JOE. Why?

MUM. Nan got a lot worse last night.

MOLLY. Worse? You mean like more ill?

MUM. A lot more ill. And her body couldn't, she couldn't get better. And so. She went to sleep and, erm, she didn't wake up.

JOE. That's not fair.

MUM. No, darling, it's not fair at all.

MOLLY. But it's her birthday next week. We've made a card with sixty-two on it.

MUM. I know, sweet.

MOLLY (*to us*). Sixty-two. I mean it's old, but it's not old-old. It's not one hundred, and loads of people live till one hundred. Sixty-two is… (*Works it out.*) thirty-eight years less than a hundred. My mum's thirty-eight. And now her mum, our nan… isn't here any more.

JOE. Just like that.

MOLLY. I go into Nan's room

JOE. Where all her things are exactly where she left them

MOLLY. And it seems so weird that she won't ever come back again

JOE. Ever.

Beat.

MOLLY. Mum starts crying

JOE. And she doesn't stop

MOLLY. She's still crying the next day

JOE. And the next day

MOLLY. She can't do anything

JOE. She has to stay in bed

MOLLY. She can't go to work

JOE. She can't read stories

MOLLY. She can't cook

JOE. She can't get dressed

MOLLY. So I do it.

JOE. Molly learns how to do all the stuff

MOLLY. I make the tea

JOE. She does the bath

MOLLY. I go to the shop and put electric on the card

JOE. She washes the clothes

MOLLY. And I dry the clothes

JOE. Molly is… Supergirl! And I am Superboy!

MOLLY. The loose-cannon helper –

JOE. Kapow! Zap!

MOLLY. Supergirl can do anything and everything – breakfast

JOE. Kapow!

MOLLY. Washing

JOE. Zap!

MOLLY. Tidying-up

JOE. Biff, bash, bang!

MOLLY. Nothing can stop Supergirl!

JOE. Molly says we can't tell anyone about Supergirl

MOLLY. Because we don't want everyone knowing our business

JOE. So we keep it a secret

MOLLY *and* JOE. Sssssh!

MOLLY. Only the thing is that Supergirl doesn't know about the Fluff Monster.

JOE. No one knows about the Fluff Monster

MOLLY. The Fluff Monster lives in the tumble dryer, and it grabs the bobbly bits of fluff off your clothes

JOE. And it eats them so it gets bigger and bigger

MOLLY. And you're supposed to take it out and clean it, get rid of it

JOE. Or it's dangerous

MOLLY. But nobody tells Supergirl that

JOE. So the Fluff Monster keeps growing

MOLLY. Getting bigger and bigger

JOE. And hotter and hotter

MOLLY. And one day it gets too hot

JOE. And the Fluff Monster decides it's had enough

MOLLY. And it sparks

JOE. And it explodes

MOLLY. And it throws out flames

    JOE *puts his hand into the fire.*

JOE. OW!

MOLLY. NO! Joe! What are you doing? Quick – put your hand in the sink –

JOE. Superboy's DOWN!

MOLLY. I take the plug out of the wall

And I soak all the tea towels I can find and throw them over the dryer

JOE. And it calms down. Phew.

MOLLY. We have to go to hospital to get a bandage on Joe's hand

JOE. Superboy's special armband – kapow –

Victory – they dance.

MOLLY. But when we get home a woman called Michelle is there

MICHELLE. Hello, Joe, hello, Molly. I'm Michelle.

MOLLY. She tells us not to worry, but –

MICHELLE. Your mum's not very well at the moment.

JOE. Is that why she can't stop crying?

MICHELLE. Yes. Your mum loves you both very much, and she wants to look after you. But she is quite poorly, so she needs to go to hospital for a little while.

JOE. I don't WANT her to go to hospital

MOLLY. And Joe starts crying

JOE. Because I don't want Mum to die

MICHELLE. That isn't going to happen, Joe. Your mum just needs to go to hospital to get the treatment she needs to get better.

JOE. So we pack our things

MOLLY. And Joe's dad Kevin comes to take Joe to stay at his house

JOE. Dad!

MOLLY. There isn't room for me at Kevin's because they've got a new baby now –

JOE. Baby Liam. My boring brother. All he does is sleep and cry and poo and –

MOLLY. But Michelle says not to worry because she knows a place –

MICHELLE. It's called Riverside. It's a really lovely place, Molly, they'll look after you while your mum gets better. And I know there's another girl there at the moment who's just your age.

MOLLY. So I kiss my mum and wave to Joe and Kevin

JOE *waves*.

And I get in Michelle's car and I go to Riverside.

And I don't cry.

JOE. Supergirl never cries.

MOLLY. Because I know that when Mum gets better everything will go back to normal.

MOLLY *closes her eyes tight*.

Music. MOLLY *and* TAYLOR *are together*.

MOLLY *is crying.* TAYLOR *has her arm around* MOLLY, *comforting her*.

Did anyone see?

TAYLOR. No! Don't worry about the Idiot Crew anyway. Everyone cries.

MOLLY. I don't.

TAYLOR. I seen Reece crying once. That time his dad never turned up. He said it was hayfever but it definitely wasn't.

MOLLY. I hate crying.

TAYLOR. Are you worried about your mum?

MOLLY. No. Well yes. (*Beat*.) I miss my nan.

TAYLOR. I miss mine. Miss her all the time. Talk to her, I do.

MOLLY. How?

TAYLOR. Just imagine that she's there, don't I? Then I just start chatting on.

MOLLY. I can't do that.

TAYLOR. Course you can. You can imagine anything.

MOLLY. Nah.

TAYLOR. I do this thing. I have this little, like, box, in my head.

MOLLY. A box?

TAYLOR. Yeah. It's red.

MOLLY. Why?

TAYLOR. Just is. It's always been red.

MOLLY. And?

TAYLOR. I'm telling you, aren't I? So it's a red box and it lives in my head, and it's where I put all the stuff that I don't want to ever forget.

MOLLY. Okay…

TAYLOR. I only save good stuff in there. All the bad stuff, I just bin that.

MOLLY. You've got a bin in your head as well?

TAYLOR. I've got a big brain.

MOLLY. So what's in your red box?

TAYLOR. My mum holding some yellow flowers. Winning the egg-and-spoon race in Reception. A dress with green and pink watermelons on it. The Rainbow Dash teddy that used to come everywhere with me till it got left at a placement and no one got round to picking it up. When you go I'll put you in it.

MOLLY (*giggling*). Me?

TAYLOR. So what I do is, I just close my eyes and concentrate dead hard, and sometimes I can imagine that all the things in the box are real, here, now. Go on, have a go. Try to imagine your nan.

MOLLY *tries. She opens her eyes, can't do it.*

MOLLY. I feel daft.

TAYLOR. Telling you, it works. So if they lose your stuff. Or if you lose someone. When you can't have the stuff you need in real life… you've got it all – up here.

TAYLOR *taps the side of* MOLLY*'s head.*

TAYLOR *is gone. Music stops.*

Alarm clock.

MOLLY. Joe! Time to get up!

JOE. I'm up I'm up I'm up –

JOE *jumps up.*

MOLLY (*calling*). S'alright, Mum, you stay there, I'll bring you a cup of tea –

MUM. Oh, thanks, love –

MOLLY. Cornflakes –

JOE. Milk –

MOLLY. Face hands teeth – Joe! Teeth!

JOE. Teeth –

MOLLY. Hair –

JOE. Uniform –

MOLLY *and* JOE. Bye, Mum!

MUM. Bye, kids!

JOE. And we're off!

They get on the bus.

BUS DRIVER. How many times, can you MOVE DOWN THE BUS, PLEASE!

MOLLY. School.

In Science when we have to get into pairs, Abi turns away from me to work with Shadia and I have to be a pair with Ms Johnson.

MS JOHNSON. Has everyone got someone? No? Don't worry, Molly, you can be my partner, you lucky thing!

MOLLY. Last bell.

Pick Joe up.

JOE. At carpet time I was being a Diplodocus and I didn't notice that everyone was already sat on the carpet till Ms Morahan said, 'We're just waiting for this dinosaur to join us,' and it was me! She really thought I was really a Diplodocus, can you believe it?

MOLLY. After school we have a catch-up with Michelle.

JOE. She gives us apple juice and as many custard creams as we want.

JOE *rams about five custard creams into his mouth.*

MICHELLE. So. How are things at home?

MOLLY *and* JOE. Good.

MICHELLE. And school?

MOLLY *and* JOE. Good.

MICHELLE. Things might be a bit strange at first.

MOLLY *and* JOE. No.

MOLLY. That's a trick and we know it.

JOE. We ain't falling for that one. Pow.

MICHELLE. It's okay if it's a bit strange?

MOLLY *and* JOE. It's not strange, it's fine.

MOLLY. On the way out Michelle pulls me to the side.

MICHELLE. Molly? I know… it can be tricky, being twelve.

MOLLY. How d'you mean?

MICHELLE. High school – lessons, homework, friends. Some people expecting you to be very grown up and some people treating you like a kid. And when there are lots of changes at home –

MOLLY. I'm fine.

MICHELLE. Okay.

MOLLY. And then we go to bed, get up and do it all again. And the next day, and the next, and the next –

Music – one of MOLLY*'s songs.* MOLLY *and* JOE *go through the motions in unison, with* MOLLY *helping* JOE.

They get out of bed, stretch, go downstairs.

MOLLY *gets their breakfast; they eat in unison.*

They wash their faces, brush their teeth.

They get dressed – shirts, trousers, then they tie their ties. MOLLY *does* JOE*'s.*

They brush their hair, then MOLLY *holds* JOE *still and does his again.*

They wave bye to MUM, *get their bags and go.*

They get on the bus, shuffle down, off the bus.

They are at school – MOLLY *working, head down, alone,* JOE *playing dinosaurs.*

The bell goes.

MOLLY *picks up* JOE, *they walk home.*

Key in the door.

They eat, brush teeth and go to bed.

They repeat this again and again.

Music fades.

And then on Friday we come home and Mum is crying

JOE. Proper crying this time

MOLLY. In bed

JOE. In the afternoon.

MOLLY. Mum?

MUM (*through tears*). Moll.

MOLLY. Are you okay?

MUM. Yeah. I'm just a little bit sad today.

MOLLY. Oh –

MUM. It's hard without her, isn't it? It's really hard.

MOLLY. Yeah. (*Beat.*) Right, Mum, you stay there, and me and Joe, we'll make the tea, yeah? All your favourite things, you just, it's alright, Mum, it'll be okay, yeah?

She turns. Back downstairs.

Open the fridge. What we got?

JOE. Bit of milk –

MOLLY. Tomatoes –

JOE. Eggs –

MOLLY. Bit of bacon –

JOE. Mayonnaise –

MOLLY. Mustard –

JOE. Jam –

MOLLY. Not jam! Right, mix it all up in a pan – careful –

JOE. I'm being careful –

MOLLY. You're getting it everywhere! Move out the way –

JOE. No!

MOLLY. Smells a bit funny –

JOE. Smells a bit horrible –

MOLLY. It'll be fine –

JOE. Plates –

MOLLY. Whooops!

JOE. Crash!

They both gasp.

MOLLY. What did you do that for?

JOE. I didn't do nothing it was the plate, jumped out my hand –

MOLLY. You better clean it up, quick –

MUM *walks in.*

JOE. You can't tell me what to do, you're not the boss of me –

MOLLY. Shut UP, JOE!

MOLLY *sees* MUM.

She stops. JOE *stops.*

MUM *looks at the mess.*

(To us.) Mum's eyes take it all in.

JOE. She bends down and picks up a piece of plate

MOLLY. It was one of Nan's old plates

JOE. That had a colourful bird picture in the middle

MOLLY. And she looks at the bit of plate closely

JOE. Then she kind of hugs it

MUM. I can't cope with this –

MOLLY. And then she turns around and goes, back to her room

JOE. Still holding the broken piece of plate

(To MOLLY.*)* Moll?

MOLLY. What?

JOE. Can I put the telly on?

MOLLY. Yeah.

JOE goes.

I can't cope with this either.

So I put my coat on.

She does.

I close the front door behind me.

And as I walk down the path, two things happen.

One – I put my hand in my coat pocket and I pull out a map.

The map that me and Taylor printed in Yvonne's office, with a green felt-tip line showing the way from mine to hers.

And two – I look up and I see Vera.

Vera, Nan's car and best friend, red and rusty and smiling at me.

MOLLY is still for a second, working it out. Then she moves into action.

I try the door.

Open!

The door opens.

And then under the mat…

She feels under the mat.

Nan's secret spare key.

MOLLY gets in to the car. She puts her seatbelt on. She adjusts the mirrors.

Come on come on come on…

She turns the key and the engine comes on.

Yes!

She gets the car in gear.

Foot, then across and up –

She sets off.

Oh my god oh my god oh my god.

JOE *giggles*.

What was that?

JOE *pops up from the back seat.*

JOE. Oh my god oh my god oh my god!

MOLLY *stops the car with a screech.*

MOLLY. Shut up, Joe! What are you doing there?

JOE. I can hear a scaredy-cat.

MOLLY. You need to get out, now.

JOE. No!

MOLLY. I'm going back to Riverside and you're not coming.

JOE. I'm not staying here without you.

MOLLY. Go back to your dad's then.

JOE. No! They don't want me there. They don't even notice me. Too busy going, 'Ooh, clever Liam, eating his porridge, ooh, clever Liam, clapping his hands' – I can eat porridge and clap and I can do a forward roll but no one cares. And I heard Helen say I was a pain in the neck.

MOLLY. You are a pain in the neck.

JOE. I'm not getting out and you can't make me.

MOLLY *looks at him. She sighs.*

MOLLY. Right, fine, put your belt on.

JOE. Yesssssssssss!

MOLLY *starts up the car.*

And we're off! Superboy and Supergirl –

MOLLY. Supergirl and Superboy and Vera –

JOE. On a fantastic adventure –

MOLLY. It's not a fantastic adventure, it's serious –

JOE. Yes, it's a serious adventure –

MOLLY. Shut up! I need to concentrate!

JOE *mimes zipping his mouth shut.*

(*To us.*) It's actually not that hard, it's actually really easy, there's nothing to it, just right foot faster, left foot gear change, left arm gears, one, two, three, four and then steering, really!

JOE. Past Brenda and her dog that's nearly bigger than her –

MOLLY. Past the house on the corner that has Christmas lights all year round –

JOE. Get to the end and we look left –

They look left.

MOLLY. And right –

They look right.

JOE. Go!

MOLLY. On to the main road

JOE. Moll?

MOLLY. What?

JOE. Hungry.

MOLLY. No way, you'll have to wait, I'm not stopping –

Beat.

JOE. Moll?

MOLLY *drives*.

Moll?

MOLLY *drives*.

MOLL!

MOLLY. What?

JOE. Starving.

MOLLY. I'm. Not. Stopping.

(*To us*.) And I'm not stopping, he can do one, as Nan would
say –

NAN. You can do one, you cheeky thing –

MOLLY. But then, when we're sitting at the traffic lights, I look
up and see it.

The big, bright, yellow 'M'.

JOE. McDONALD'S.

MOLLY. MACCIE D'S.

MOLLY (*to us*). You know how you can smell McDonald's
chips from miles away? And we've had no tea...

They both smell the air.

JOE. Can we, can we, can we, can we?

MOLLY. No money.

(*To us*.) And so we're sitting there, sniffing the chips and
waiting for the lights to change –

JOE. And outside it's getting really windy

MOLLY. Leaves blowing across the front of the car

JOE. And then a leaf gets stuck on Vera

MOLLY. Right there on the windscreen

JOE. Only it's not a leaf

MOLLY. It's a piece of paper

JOE. With writing on it

They both peer, turning their heads almost upside down to read it.

MOLLY *and* JOE. 'Today only. Free Happy Meals.'

They look at each other. JOE *winds the window down, reaches out and grabs the voucher.*

Behind them the cars start beeping.

MOLLY (*to* JOE). Hold on tight – (*To us.*) So I spin the wheel and we screech into the drive-thru.

A crackly VOICE *speaks from nowhere making* MOLLY *jump.*

VOICE. HELLO, WELCOME TO McDONALD'S. CAN I TAKE YOUR ORDER?

JOE. Two Chicken Nugget Happy Meals please –

VOICE. IS THAT YOUR ORDER COMPLETE? DRIVE ROUND TO THE FIRST WINDOW PLEASE.

MOLLY. We drive to the first window.

ASSISTANT. That's four ninety-eight, please –

MOLLY (*to us*). So I hand over the piece of paper. We both stare straight ahead.

MOLLY *and* JOE *stare straight ahead. The* ASSISTANT *inspects the voucher.*

JOE. Holding our breath

MOLLY. And then

ASSISTANT. Drive to the next window to collect your food.

JOE. Can you believe that?!

ASSISTANT. Two Happy Meals, enjoy!

MOLLY (*to us*). So we eat the nuggets

JOE. And the chips

MOLLY. Pulled up outside the swimming baths

JOE. And it's dead exciting

MOLLY. Being out at night when it's getting dark and we should be in bed. Then Joe goes:

JOE. Wouldn't you love to go in there?

MOLLY. He's staring straight ahead through the window of the swimming baths, all blue and empty.

JOE. Whenever I go past it at night when it's all closed and shut, I wish I could just jump in, when no one else is there – have a go on the diving board that you aren't allowed on.

MOLLY. Yeah.

JOE. Why do they even have a diving board if no one's allowed on it?

MOLLY *has an idea.*

Beat.

MOLLY. Finish your chips.

(*To us.*) And before I know what I'm doing, we're getting out of the car and creeping along the side of the baths.

JOE. Superboy and Supergirl and Vera on a fantastic, serious adventure –

MOLLY. We get to the fire door and it opens

JOE. And the cleaner comes out. Duck!

They duck behind the door. The CLEANER *comes out. She lights a cigarette, chatting on her mobile phone.*

CLEANER. Oh aye, well, I'm nearly finished here, so I'll not be long. Just give the bogs a quick once-over –

MOLLY. She can't see us through the cloud of smoke as we creep past her and in.

JOE. The water is absolutely still. With the diving board high at one end.

MOLLY *and* JOE *look at each other, then nod.*

MOLLY. We climb the steps at either side of the board

JOE. It's a race and I'm winning

MOLLY. He is not! We get to the top at exactly the same time –

JOE. Then we run to the edge of the board – whoa –

They both stop at the edge of the board.

MOLLY. It's a long way down –

JOE. Scaredy-cat –

MOLLY. Am not –

JOE. Prove it.

MOLLY. After three –

JOE. One –

MOLLY. Two –

JOE. Three –

MOLLY. And we jump over the side and we're falling –

JOE. Diving –

MOLLY. The air rushing past our faces –

JOE. And then

MOLLY. We hit the water –

They both make a SPLASH sound.

JOE. And we race to the other end –

MOLLY. Joe's first twenty-five metres!

JOE. And we're neck and neck

MOLLY. Our hands reach the side at exactly the same time

JOE. And we pull ourselves out

MOLLY. I won!

JOE. No I won!

MOLLY. And there's the cleaner, standing in front of us with her mouth open –

CLEANER. Oi!

JOE. So we run around her

MOLLY. Back out the fire exit

JOE. Soaking wet

MOLLY. Come on come on come on –

JOE. Vera fires up –

MOLLY. And we're off!

JOE. With the cleaner standing behind us with her mouth still open

MOLLY. Did you see her face? (*Beat.*) Hold the map, will you?

(*To us.*) We set off to Riverside with the windows open to dry our clothes. Joe keeps getting sleepy and letting the map droop over – Joe! I can't see! Hold it up!

JOE. My hand hurts!

MOLLY (*to us*). But in the end I realise I know the way, I remember the roads, and the trees, and the colours on the buildings and even in the dark, I can get us there, and before I know it Vera's headlights are shining up at a medium-sized building, kind of like a cross between a house and a tiny school. All dark except for one light in the bottom window where there are five heart-shaped stickers stuck to the glass in the shape of a 'T'.

(*To* JOE.) This is it.

Nothing.

Joe? We're here.

Joe?

She looks back into the backseat. JOE *is asleep.*

Typical.

MOLLY *looks up at Riverside. She steels herself, then gets out of the car.*

Freezing.

MOLLY *looks up at* TAYLOR*'s window.*

(*Loud whisper.*) Taylor?

Nothing.

Taylor?

Nothing. MOLLY *goes to the window and taps, a special pattern to the rhythm of 'Shake It Off'.*

(*Sings.*) Players gonna play play play play play –

(*To us, whisper.*) That's our special tap. Has to be quiet so no one hears, has to be exactly the same every time so you know it's not one of the boys tricking you.

She waits.

Nothing.

She taps again, steps back, closes her eyes, crosses her fingers and waits.

After a moment, she opens her eyes and uncrosses her fingers.

She's not coming, is she?

She's probably asleep.

She might have moved to a new placement.

She might have forgotten me.

TAYLOR *appears.*

TAYLOR. Moll?

MOLLY. Taylor!

TAYLOR *runs to* MOLLY.

'Shake It Off' starts up. They dance their routine. It's great, they are both really into it, it's their language, their way of talking to each other.

The music stops and they stop. They look at each other.

TAYLOR. Can't believe it's really you! You came back!

MOLLY. I promised, didn't I?

TAYLOR. Yeah, but I didn't think you actually would. People say that they'll come back but they never do.

MOLLY. Well – here I am. I'm back.

TAYLOR. You're staying?

MOLLY. Yeah, if they'll let me. But I can just hide in your room for tonight, can't I?

TAYLOR. Totally. How did you even get here?

MOLLY. Vera brought me, didn't she?

TAYLOR. Who the frig's Vera?!

MOLLY. My nan's car.

TAYLOR (*laughing*). You're off your head, mate!

MOLLY. I know I am.

They laugh – for a second it's like it used to be.

A light switches on upstairs. They both freeze, look up and then at each other.

TAYLOR. Quick, get inside before someone clocks us.

MOLLY. Yeah. Oh wait.

TAYLOR. What?

MOLLY (*sigh*). Joe. I can't leave him out here.

TAYLOR. Joe?

MOLLY. He fell asleep in the car.

TAYLOR. You brought your little brother?

MOLLY. I didn't want to. He just... came.

TAYLOR *crosses her arms, looks at* MOLLY. *Beat.*

TAYLOR. So you're not staying.

MOLLY. Yeah I am.

TAYLOR. You've got your baby brother with you –

MOLLY. So?

TAYLOR. – you've brought your nan's old car which you'll defo have to take back –

MOLLY. No I won't, Mum doesn't even want her any more –

TAYLOR. – you've got no bags or nothing with you... you don't really want to come back here, you're just running away.

MOLLY. I'm not.

TAYLOR. Grow up, Molly. You can't just decide to put yourself back in care. It doesn't work like that. You've got a mum.

MOLLY. But I still need you! You're the only person who gets it. And now you're not there any more, and Nan isn't there any more, and I can't do the red-box thing, I've tried –

TAYLOR. It doesn't have to be red. It doesn't have to be a box. It's just a way of holding on to people when they aren't with you any more. It's just a thing that helps me, that's all.

MOLLY. I can't do it.

TAYLOR. You're doing it right now.

MOLLY. Am I?

TAYLOR. You're lucky, Moll. You don't need a red box. You've got a family. Talk to them about your nan.

MOLLY. How can I talk to my mum about Nan without making her sad again? How can I tell her what I'm worried about when what I'm worried about is her?

TAYLOR. Try.

Beat. They look at each other.

MOLLY. We are still best friends, aren't we?

TAYLOR. Course.

MOLLY. Will you be okay?

TAYLOR. Always.

She puts her finger to her head and taps it. MOLLY *nods.*

MOLLY. Maybe one day you'll go back to live with your mum.

TAYLOR. Yeah, maybe.

MOLLY. I'll come back and see you. I know the way now, so…

TAYLOR. You better had.

They hug, then TAYLOR *disappears.*

MOLLY (*to us*). And she's completely gone. It's just me, and Vera, and Joe asleep in the back.

And then through the dark, I see someone standing next to the car.

NAN *appears.*

Nan!

NAN. Come on, Molly Daydream, don't just stand there, it's the middle of the night, Vera needs her beauty sleep, don't you, pet? Hop in the back and let's get going.

MOLLY. And so I do. I climb into the back seat with Joe and Nan tucks us under a blanket and Vera and Nan drive us all back home, through the stars and the streetlights, and I close my eyes and I go to sleep.

Music.

JOE *and* MOLLY *are asleep on the back seat of the car.*

The stars light them.

A noise, maybe an owl.

They stir.

MOLLY *opens one eye.*

JOE *opens one eye.*

They both open their eyes and look at each other.

Ugh! Have you been dribbling on me?

JOE. No! (*Beat.*) Actually, yeah…

MOLLY. Ugh. Where are we…?

JOE. Home! Look –

He points to the house.

MOLLY. Oh yeah. (*To us.*) And we are. We climb out of the car.

They stretch.

It's the middle of the night and we're standing outside a house.

JOE. Our house.

MOLLY. It looks just the same.

JOE. There's my green scooter

MOLLY. The broken blue gate

JOE. The grey curtains

MOLLY. The red door

JOE. The door opens

MOLLY *and* JOE. Mum!

MUM. Molly! Joe!

MOLLY. She isn't crying now

JOE. She's extremely extremely angry

MUM. Where the hell have you been?

MOLLY. We were just in the car –

JOE. Yeah, we went on this fantastic adventure –

MOLLY *shoots him a look.*

MOLLY. Yeah just sitting in the car really. And then we fell asleep. Sorry.

MUM. You've been *in the car*? You've been out here, in the dark, *hiding*, while I've been going out of my mind with worry, looking for you? I'm so mad I can't even *look* at you! Get inside, get up to your rooms, go on –

MOLLY (*to us*). We go upstairs and sit on the edge of my bed.

I can't remember when Mum last shouted at us like that

JOE (*to us*). Me either

MOLLY. And even though it's bad it's kind of –

JOE. Funny –

JOE *giggles.*

MOLLY *giggles.*

MOLLY. Ssssh! She's coming –

They can't stop laughing. MUM *enters.*

MUM (*noticing their laughter*). Do you think this is funny?

MOLLY. No! We're not laughing, we're just –

JOE. It did feel a tiny bit funny

MUM. Did it?

MOLLY. Because you hadn't shouted at us for a long time, it felt a bit strange and a bit like we were little kids again –

(*To us.*) And then something really weird happens. The laugh in my head and in my mouth and my throat suddenly changes into –

MOLLY *starts to cry.*

Into –

She tries to stop crying but can't.

Into –

JOE. Why are you crying?

MUM. Molly?

MOLLY. I'm not crying!

(To us.) Supergirl never cries.

MUM *goes to* MOLLY.

MUM. It's alright! Sweet, Mum's here, it's okay. Don't cry.

MOLLY. But now I've started I can't stop, the tears keep coming and coming and there's nothing I can do to stop them.

MUM. What is it, Moll?

MOLLY *(to us)*. So I try.

(To MUM.*)* Nothing's the same.

Beat.

MUM. Okay…

MOLLY. And I'm worried all the time.

MUM. What about?

MOLLY. About everything. About you. And now Nan's gone and I've tried to do what Nan would do but it's no good.

MUM. I see. *(Beat.)* And Joe, do you feel worried too?

JOE. Bit. You were crying.

MOLLY. And you said you couldn't cope.

MUM. It's been hard for all of us, the last week or so, hasn't it? Getting used to being here again. There've been a lot of changes. Molly's right – things aren't the same. I was upset because I miss Nan. And sometimes I see things that remind me of her, like the cake programme on the telly, or Vera, and it makes me sad that she isn't here.

MOLLY. Me too.

JOE. Me three.

MUM. But even though I'm sad sometimes, I'm happy too. I'm happy to have you two back at home and I'm happy that you're safe and I'm looking forward to all the fun we can have together tomorrow and the next day and the next. And I'm learning to cope with the sad feelings, so that they don't take over the happy feelings too much. Does that make sense?

MOLLY *and* JOE *look at each other.*

MOLLY (*to* MUM). I don't think I'll ever be able to stop worrying ever again.

MUM. Come here.

MUM *hugs* MOLLY *and then* JOE *to her. She holds on to their hands.*

I wish I could take away all your worries. But I can't.

Just like you can't take away my worries.

Beat.

MOLLY. Mum puts us to bed.

It's so late it's getting light.

MUM. A story from a book or one from Mum's head?

JOE. Mum's head!

MUM. Okay, here goes. Once upon a time, Mum and Molly and Joe and Vera went off for an adventure –

JOE. And got a free McDonald's in the drive-thru!

MUM. Erm, well, I don't think that would happen but okay, if you like –

MOLLY (*to us*). And – do you know what? I feel comfy in my bed for the first time all week.

MUM. ... and they all went home to bed. The End. Okay, kids. That's your lot. Joe, you jump into bed. And in the morning

we could go for that McDonald's, if you like? Maybe go
swimming as well? Do us good.

JOE. Yesss.

JOE *goes into his room.*

MOLLY. And just before I fall asleep, I realise that Taylor was
right. I talked to my mum and somehow that took the worm
bit out of the worry.

TAYLOR. See? You've got to hold on to people.

MOLLY. Told you. She really is a magical kind of person,
Taylor.

And then I close my eyes again and I fall fast asleep.

End.

A Nick Hern Book

How To Be A Kid first published in Great Britain in 2017 as a paperback original by Nick Hern Books Limited, The Glasshouse, 49a Goldhawk Road, London W12 8QP, in association with Paines Plough, Theatr Clwyd and the Orange Tree Theatre, Richmond

How To Be A Kid copyright © 2017 Sarah McDonald-Hughes

Cover photography: Rebecca Need-Meaner

Designed and typeset by Nick Hern Books, London
Printed in the UK by Mimeo Ltd, Huntingdon, Cambridgeshire PE29 6XX

A CIP catalogue record for this book is available from the British Library

ISBN 978 1 84842 704 4

Other Plays for Young People to Perform from Nick Hern Books

Original Plays

100
Christopher Heimann,
Neil Monaghan, Diene Petterle

BANANA BOYS
Evan Placey

BLOOD AND ICE
Liz Lochhead

BOYS
Ella Hickson

BRAINSTORM
Ned Glasier, Emily Lim and Company Three

BUNNY
Jack Thorne

BURYING YOUR BROTHER IN THE PAVEMENT
Jack Thorne

CHRISTMAS IS MILES AWAY
Chloë Moss

COCKROACH
Sam Holcroft

DISCO PIGS
Enda Walsh

EIGHT
Ella Hickson

THE FALL
James Fritz

GIRLS LIKE THAT
Evan Placey

HOLLOWAY JONES
Evan Placey

I CAUGHT CRABS IN WALBERSWICK
Joel Horwood

MOGADISHU
Vivienne Franzmann

MOTH
Declan Greene

THE MYSTAE
Nick Whitby

OVERSPILL
Ali Taylor

PRONOUN
Evan Placey

SAME
Deborah Bruce

THERE IS A WAR
Tom Basden

THE URBAN GIRL'S GUIDE TO CAMPING AND OTHER PLAYS
Fin Kennedy

THE WARDROBE
Sam Holcroft

Adaptations

ANIMAL FARM
Ian Wooldridge
Adapted from George Orwell

ARABIAN NIGHTS
Dominic Cooke

BEAUTY AND THE BEAST
Laurence Boswell

CORAM BOY
Helen Edmundson
Adapted from Jamila Gavin

DAVID COPPERFIELD
Alastair Cording
Adapted from Charles Dickens

GREAT EXPECTATIONS
Nick Ormerod and Declan Donnellan
Adapted from Charles Dickens

HIS DARK MATERIALS
Nicholas Wright
Adapted from Philip Pullman

THE JUNGLE BOOK
Stuart Paterson
Adapted from Rudyard Kipling

KENSUKE'S KINGDOM
Stuart Paterson
Adapted from Michael Morpurgo

KES
Lawrence Till
Adapted from Barry Hines

NOUGHTS & CROSSES
Dominic Cooke
Adapted from Malorie Blackman

THE RAILWAY CHILDREN
Mike Kenny
Adapted from E. Nesbit

SWALLOWS AND AMAZONS
Helen Edmundson and Neil Hannon
Adapted from Arthur Ransome

TO SIR, WITH LOVE
Ayub Khan-Din
Adapted from E.R Braithwaite

TREASURE ISLAND
Stuart Paterson
Adapted from Robert Louis Stevenson

WENDY & PETER PAN
Ella Hickson
Adapted from J.M. Barrie

THE WOLVES OF WILLOUGHBY CHASE
Russ Tunney
Adapted from Joan Aiken

For more information on plays to perform visit
www.nickhernbooks.co.uk/plays-to-perform